THIS

# ALCHEMY
# JOURNAL

BELONGS TO

_____

# ON JOURNALING AS ALCHEMY

I reach for the page like I reach for prayer: to plead, to confess, to commune, to remember that all is not chaos, all is not lost.

I reach for it like a reporter's pad: to record something overheard, something glimpsed, some stray thought I don't want to forget.

I reach for it like a friend: for company, for counsel. I tell my journal what knots I'm in, and together we untangle the threads.

I make of this writing a ritual: to mark the thresholds, to traverse the valleys and the peaks, to honor the space between no longer and not yet.

The journal is oceanic. It is capacious. It is memory, reverie, distillation, transformation. It teaches me to pay attention, to see the world anew, to rearrange the pieces, to play.

The journal is tabula rasa and terra incognita. It is a mirror for the self—past, present, and future—and a portal onto the not yet known.

The journal is refuge: a hiding place, a searching place, a finding place. It's where I go to know myself, to uncover the unlived lives within me.

Here I call in alchemy. Here I create myself. Here I write my way through.

164

# INDEX

| PAGE Nº | TOPIC |
|---------|-------|
|         |       |

# INDEX

| PAGE № | TOPIC |
| --- | --- |
| | |

# INDEX

| PAGE Nº | TOPIC |
| --- | --- |
| | |

*For more journaling inspiration and prompts,*
*visit theisolationjournals.com and get the companion book,*

# The Book of Alchemy:
## A Creative Practice for an Inspired Life

*by* Suleika Jaouad

Hardcover ISBN 979-8-217-15397-8

Printed in Malaysia

2 4 6 8 9 7 5 3 1

FIRST EDITION

BOOK TEAM: Production editor: Andy Lefkowitz • Managing editor: Rebecca Berlant •
Production manager: Linnea Knollmueller

The authorized representative in the EU for product safety and compliance
is Penguin Random House Ireland, Morrison Chambers, 32 Nassau Street,
Dublin D02 YH68, Ireland. https://eu-contact.penguin.ie

For more journaling inspiration and prompts, get the companion book,
*The Book of Alchemy: A Creative Practice for an Inspired Life*
by Suleika Jaouad and visit theisolationjournals.com.